Waldo, Tell Me Where's Grandpa?

Series

Published by The Regina Press, Melville, New York 11747

ISBN 088271 473 2

Printed in Belgium

Waldo, Tell Me Where's Grandpa

by Hans Wilhelm

Regina Press
New York

To Peter Klesy

One morning Michael's mother woke Michael very softly and told him that his grandpa had died during the night.

Michael knew that Grandpa had been ill for quite a while. Michael reached for his Teddy. He felt strange.

Michael went up to Grandpa's room. It had been empty for some time. He climbed onto Grandpa's chair. It felt cold. Would Grandpa never come back?

Then the door opened. It was Waldo—Michael's best friend. "I thought I would find you here," said Waldo.

"Oh, Waldo," said Michael, "why did Grandpa have to die?"

Waldo put his arms around his friend and then said, "Grandpa lives, Michael. He just no longer lives here on earth."

"What do you mean?" asked Michael, "Where did he go?"

"Come," said Waldo, "I'll try to explain it to you." He picked up Michael and they both sat on Grandpa's bed.

"Every person is a child of God, our Father," began Waldo. "You, your mother, your father and Grandpa are all children of God. Now, every child of God has 'a soul.' And when your soul lives here on earth it has a house, or a shell which is your own body."

"You mean that inside my own body there is my soul?" asked Michael.

"Yes," said Waldo. "And *you* are that soul. *You* are that child of God who lives inside your body."

"All of God's children," Waldo added, "live forever. But their bodies here on earth don't last very long. Bodies get old, break, wear out, get very ill or have a terrible accident. Then the soul slips out of the broken body and leaves it behind. Think of the beautiful butterfly that leaves behind its empty cocoon."

"Is that what happened to Grandpa?" asked Michael after a little pause.

"Yes," said Waldo. "When Grandpa died his soul left his earthly body to return to the Kingdom of God, from where he once came. It is something very natural and very wonderful! It's nothing to be afraid of," said Waldo quietly.

"But where is Grandpa now?" Michael wanted to know.

"His soul is now on the way back home to God, his Father." said Waldo. "He may even meet up with his friends and relatives who have gone before him. They may even throw a great welcoming party for him!"

"Wow!" said Michael. "Will he see Christ?" Michael knew that Christ was God's son and looked after him and his family.

"I should hope so," said Waldo. "Christ will continue to care for Grandpa."

"But," said Michael—and suddenly some tears shot to his eyes. "But why can't Grandpa stay here with us? I miss him. He was my best friend— after you," he quickly added and more tears flowed.

"I know," said Waldo. "It's very difficult for all of us. He was a great grandpa and life without him will be very different. We will miss him a lot and it is sad for us. But we want to think of Grandpa. He is beginning a new adventure. And we want to wish him well."

Michael wiped off some tears. "But I wish I could talk to him. I want to ask him how he is and tell him that I love him."

"Michael, he knows that. You've told him that so many times—in so many ways. Grandpa hasn't forgotten."

"But still," said Michael, "I'd like to tell him one more time. And..." he paused, "and I also want to tell him that I'm sorry that..."

"What?" asked Waldo.

"I want to tell him that I'm sorry
that I trampled down all the flowers
in his flower bed. I never told him so."

Waldo smiled and gave Michael a special hug, "If that is so important to you, then you can ask Christ to tell him. In fact, I have an idea. Why don't you write it in a letter?"

"A letter?" asked Michael. "But where shall I send it?"

"Well, you wouldn't have to actually mail it," said Waldo. "Christ will know what you have written because He is always with you. And He'll share it with Grandpa. Trust Him."

"Are you sure?"

"Of course I'm sure. Christ will help you. He doesn't want you to feel sad because Grandpa is gone. He wants you to send Grandpa all your love and happy thoughts."

"I'll try," said Michael as he slid off the bed. It looked like Michael was beginning to feel a little better.

Michael got some pencils and a piece of paper. He thought for a moment and then began to write:

DEAR CHRIST,
PLEASE TELL GRANDPA THAT i LOVE HiM.
i HOPE HE iS ALL RiGHT. HAS HE MET
SOME ANGELS?

i REALLY MiSS HiM A LOT, BUT i'M
GOING TO BE FINE. HE MUST NOT
WORRY ABOUT ME. PLEASE TE'
HiM THAT i'M SORRY THAT i
TRAMPLED DOWN ALL HiS
FLOWERS.

PLEASE GiVE MY LOVE TO
GRANDPA. i LOVE YOU, TOO

MiCHAEL

P.S. ALSO, LOVE FRO'
WALDO

And then Michael drew a picture
of a huge dinosaur on his letter.
Dinosaurs were the best thing he
could draw. And Grandpa always
loved his dinosaur pictures.

"Here, you can read it." Michael gave Waldo his letter.

Waldo read it and said, "I think this is a wonderful letter. And how do you feel now? Still sad?"

"A little," said Michael, "but not like crying anymore. I feel that Grandpa is all right. And do you think I could keep his hat and his photos to remember him by?"

"Oh yes, Michael," said Waldo. "And Grandpa gave you many other wonderful gifts, too."

"What?" asked Michael.

"Remember how he showed you how to play checkers? Remember the stories he read to you? And how he helped you build the model airplane and taught you how to skate?

"These are all great gifts," said Waldo. "Maybe one day you'll give them to your own grandchildren."

"Grandpa's greatest gift of all,"
Waldo added, "is the love we shared
with him and the love he still has for
us…which will live forever. Grandpa
is loving you right now. He will
always love you."

"I know, Waldo," said Michael,"
and I love him too, forever."

A Note About the Author

Writer, illustrator and lecturer, Hans Wilhelm, has created more than 100 children's books, which have been published around the world. His books have received many awards and honors. Hans Wilhelm, a native of Bremen, Germany, now lives in Westport, Connecticut.